# KNOWLEDGE ENCYCLOPEDIA
# FORCE & MOVEMENT

© Wonder House Books 2022

All rights reserved. No part of this book may be reproduced or transmitted in any form by any means, electronic or mechanical, including photocopying and recording, or by any information storage and retrieval system except as may be expressly permitted in writing by the publisher.

(An imprint of Prakash Books)

contact@wonderhousebooks.com

**Disclaimer:** The information contained in this encyclopedia has been collated with inputs from subject experts. All information contained herein is true to the best of the Publisher's knowledge.

ISBN : 9789354401763

# Table of Contents

| | |
|---|---|
| The Basis of the Universe | 3 |
| Force: Making Things Move | 4–5 |
| What Makes Us Move | 6–7 |
| What We are Made Of | 8–9 |
| When Things Move in a Straight Line | 10–11 |
| When Things Don't Move in a Straight Line | 12–13 |
| How the Planets Move | 14–15 |
| Why Things Fall Down | 16–17 |
| Forces of Resistance | 18–19 |
| Machines | 20–21 |
| Density and Buoyancy | 22–23 |
| Engines | 24–25 |
| Flight | 26–27 |
| To Space | 28–29 |
| The Metric System | 30–31 |
| Word Check | 32 |

# THE BASIS OF THE UNIVERSE

**Our Universe is made of two things—matter and energy.** Matter is all that you can touch, feel and see. Energy is what makes things move and work. Both matter and energy are made of tiny particles. Matter is made of atoms, which are themselves made of electrons, protons and neutrons. Protons and neutrons are made of tinier particles called quarks, which are made of tinier particles themselves.

Energy is made of tiny weightless photons. When energy meets matter, like when you kick a ball or shine a flashlight onto something, it makes matter move. When you kick a ball, the potential energy in your foot creates a mechanical force on the ball and drives it towards the goal. When light falls on the atoms of an object, the photons in it make the electrons in the atoms move and therefore produce a tiny electromagnetic force. You cannot feel this force, but you can see this as the 'shine' on the object.

This book will help you understand what force and movement are, and why the Universe is the way it is. On the way you will understand how machines work; how rockets take off; why planes don't fall from the sky; and even how the planets move in their orbits around the Sun.

▶ *Gears, which are part of many engines, help to make a small force do a lot of work*

# Force: Making Things Move

**Force is what makes things move.** It may be a giant planet revolving around giant stars; your mother dragging you out of bed to go to school; or it might be electrons jumping from one atom to another, causing a chemical reaction. It may even go right down to the fundamental particles of the Universe, pulling and pushing each other to make the vast fabric of space and time.

But science is more specific. Force, according to science, is an entity that creates motion *in a specific direction*. It is, therefore, a **vector** quantity. Your body **experiences** weight due to the force of the Earth always pulling you downwards. On the other hand, your body **possesses** mass—the total number of atoms and molecules that make you up. This is a **scalar** quantity, because you have the same mass whichever way you are headed. All measurements in physics are determined based on whether they are vectors or scalars.

## Types of Force

The Universe has four fundamental forces. With these forces, you can explain almost anything that is going on.

The first of these is gravity, the force that makes two bodies attract each other.

▼ *Modern physics understands gravity as a distortion of space-time by large bodies*

▼ *Electromagnetism is a force that explains electricity, magnetism, heat, and light*

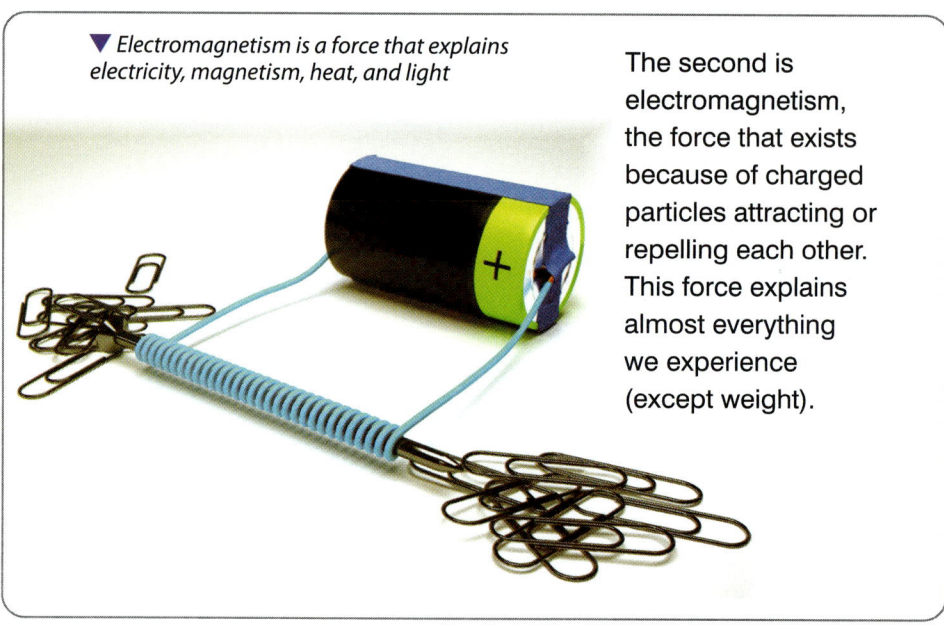

The second is electromagnetism, the force that exists because of charged particles attracting or repelling each other. This force explains almost everything we experience (except weight).

The third force is a strong force, also called the strong nuclear interaction. The force holds protons and neutrons together in a nucleus.

▼ *The strong and weak forces work at the level of the nucleus; electromagnetic force works on atomic scales; and gravity works at the galactic level*

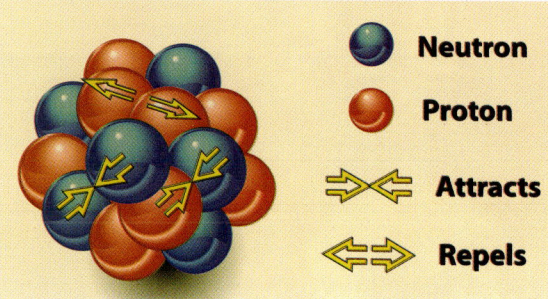

The fourth is the weak force, or the weak nuclear interaction. This also works only inside an atom's nucleus. Without this force, nuclear fusion would be difficult and stars, such as the Sun, would not exist. The continued study of these two forces will only lead to a greater understanding of natural mechanics and the universe.

SCIENCE | FORCE & MOVEMENT | 5

## Momentum

**Momentum** (symbol p) is what a body with some mass (symbol m) has when it has no force acting on it. When an object is standing still, that is, when it has no **velocity** (v), its momentum is zero. When it has some velocity, its momentum has a value. A small object at high speed (a ball hit by a bat) and a large object at low speed (a roadroller) may share the same momentum.

$$p = mv$$

▶ It takes a lot of force to change a roadroller's momentum

## Mechanical Force

In mechanical terms, force (symbol f) is the change in momentum with respect to time (symbol t). A catcher stops a ball with a small mass, whereas it takes something huge to stop a roadroller. The force may be electrical (like charges repel, opposite charges attract), magnetic (like poles repel, opposite poles attract), or it may be a property of the density and hardness of the material (friction, elasticity, etc.).

$$f = \frac{mv}{t}$$

The value v/t gives you another fundamental idea of physics: acceleration, or the rate of change of velocity with time. Force can then be expressed as a measure of the mass of an object, and the change it undergoes in its acceleration when the object meets the force.

$$f = ma$$

▼ The dog's mass and forward acceleration stop the balls' momentum

# What Makes Us Move

**Force changes the momentum of an object and therefore changes it from one state of inertia to another (inertia means a body remaining in the same state, whether moving or staying still).** This change of inertia can be used to make the device do work that is useful to us, such as using the force of your feet to pedal a bicycle. But what produces that force in the first place?

▲ *All the energy we use ultimately comes from nuclear reactions in the Sun*

It is **energy**. It is the same thing that you get by eating food, or a car gets from its fuel. All the energy on our planet ultimately comes from the Sun, which gets its energy through nuclear fission. It takes a lot to explain energy, but we can share two interesting things:

- Energy is related to mass by Albert Einstein's famous Theory of Special Relativity.

- Energy can neither be created nor destroyed, but only converted from one form to another. This is the Law of Conservation of Energy.

## Work

The conversion of energy, from one form to another, results in some work being done. When you ride a bicycle, your body uses some of the chemical energy it got from food. Your muscles turn the chemical energy to kinetic energy, and this creates the force that pushes the pedal. In physics, the total work done (W) can be explained as the distance the bicycle travelled multiplied by the total force (f) that you applied. But remember that force is a vector. Therefore, the distance that matters is the **displacement** (symbol s), which is the linear distance between the starting point and the ending point, and not the path you have travelled.

$$W = fs$$

Work is of two types—**internal** and **external**. Your heartbeat is an example of internal work; you do external work when bicycling. In internal work, all the energy is spent in keeping the system going (like your body), while in external work, the energy spent makes the body do something, like pushing the bike's pedals.

### Isn't It Amazing!

Scientists have a short way of writing extremely large numbers. So, instead of writing our planet's mass as 598,000,000,000,000,000,000,000,000 kg, we can write it as $5.98 \times 10^{24}$ kg. The number written as superscript on 10 tells you the **order of magnitude**.

▶ *The Sun delivers $3.6 \times 10^{26}$ kgm²/s³ of power every second. This unit can be further simplified as Joules per second or Watts*

WATER    SOLAR    WIND

SCIENCE | FORCE & MOVEMENT

# Potential and Kinetic Energy

**Kinetic energy** is the energy a system has when it is moving or doing work (the energy your leg has while pedalling a bicycle). If an object is at rest then it doesn't have kinetic energy. **Potential energy** is the energy available to a system due to inertia (e.g. the unspent energy from your food), or the energy it is transferring as it does work (the energy that is now part of your bicycle's inertia of movement). Sadly, your bicycle won't have much of this kinetic energy left by the end of the journey, since most will be lost due to **friction** with the ground.

▶ The relation between work and energy. The units of both are written as Newton-metres or Joules

# Power

If you look at electric batteries or lights, they are denoted by the power (symbol P) that they deliver. Something is powerful when it gives a lot of energy (which you experience as force) in a small amount of time, like a wrestler bending a bar of iron. Physicists write power as the rate at which a machine can do work (W) in each unit of time (t), usually seconds.

$$P = \frac{W}{t}$$

◀ Types of energy. We often talk of energy in terms of anything that can be converted into electricity

FOSSIL        NUCLEAR

## In Real Life

When James Watt (1736–1819) tried to sell his improved steam engine to mills, they could not understand how it would do more work than the horses they used to pull loads. Being a clever physicist, Watt denoted the energy his engine could deliver every minute (power) in terms of the amount of work a horse could do per minute. The mill owners were impressed, and that's how we got the unit we still use: horsepower.

▲ One horsepower is how much a healthy, untired horse can draw: 33,000 pounds by a foot every minute

# What We are Made Of

**Matter is the part that makes up the Universe.** It means something that has **mass**, that is, it can be touched or felt. Matter is made of protons, electrons, and neutrons, which are themselves made of tinier (subatomic) particles called quarks. Albert Einstein's Special Theory of Relativity redefines matter as a form of energy (e). His equation for it has probably become the most famous equation in the world:

$$e = mc^2$$

Where c is the velocity of light in vacuum and m is its mass. Matter is of two types:

- **Light matter**, which interacts with photons and can be perceived by us either directly (like a football), or by using scientific instruments (for particles such as quarks).

- **Dark matter**, which does not interact with photons. We cannot perceive it at all, but we know it exists because it exerts gravity. Dark matter makes up 27% of the Universe.

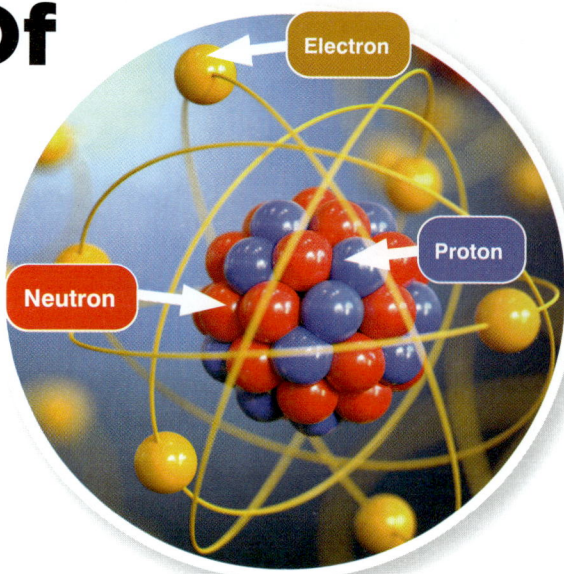

▲ *Matter is made of subatomic particles, which make up electrons, protons and neutrons, which in turn make atoms*

## Mass and Weight

The definition of mass (symbol m), useful to us in daily life, is that it is the amount of **inertia** that an object has. This is in turn proportional to the number of atoms and molecules in it (i.e. **density**) and the atomic or molecular mass of the elements and compounds it is made of. If you see two boxes of the same size on a table, how would you know which has more mass? You'd have to apply a force, by either pushing or lifting them.

**Weight** is how our bodies experience mass. In physical terms, the Earth exerts the force upon us. So, by the definition of force, your weight is your mass multiplied by the acceleration due to gravity (g). This lead to the SI unit for weight being Newtons. If your mass is 34 kg, your weight will be 34 × 9.8 kgm/s², which is 333.2 Newtons.

▼ *Weight (the gravitational pull of the Earth) is how we measure mass on a weighing balance*

### Isn't It Amazing!

Your weight (but not mass) will be different on different planets, because they have different accelerations due to gravity (g). If you weigh 333.2 Newtons on Earth, you'll only weigh 55.3 Newtons on the Moon, but 842.3 Newtons on Jupiter.

▲ *If you ever managed to land on Pluto, you would weigh only 22.3 Newtons (you would still be 34 kg though)*

SCIENCE | FORCE & MOVEMENT | 9

# Cohesion

Cohesion refers to the forces that stop things from breaking apart. There are two main forces that hold things together:

1. Ionic attraction: Salts, acids, and alkalis are materials made of ions which have opposite electric charges. Ions of opposite charge attract each other strongly and those of the same charge repel each other. In a solid state, these ions form themselves in a repeating **lattice** of alternating positive and negative charges. The attraction is strong and it takes a lot of energy (heat or mechanical) to break them. That's why things made of metal are so strong.

2. Electric dipole: Substances that are not ionic still have weak dipoles—tiny electrical charges (called $\delta+$ and $\delta-$) at each end of the molecule. The dipoles create weak attraction between different molecules, which keep them together. It takes less energy to break these forces, which are also called **van der Waals forces**. Cake is held together by such forces, which is why it crumbles so easily.

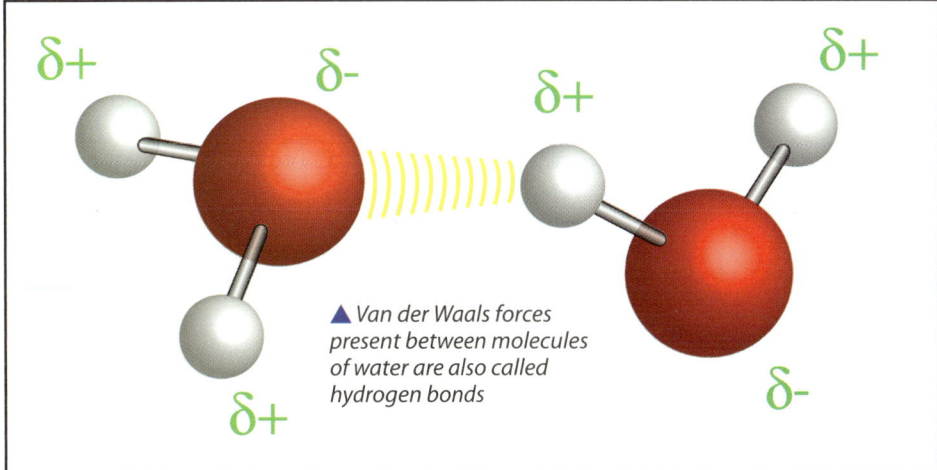

▲ Van der Waals forces present between molecules of water are also called hydrogen bonds

# Normal Force

When standing or moving on a bridge, you experience three forces:

- the **frictional force**, that is, the force required to move you;
- your weight (force due to gravity); and
- the **normal force** that acts at right angles to friction.

The normal force is the force exerted by the cohesion of the bridge on you, without which you would crash through it.

▶ A bridge's normal force depends on the density of the materials it is made of

# When Things Move in a Straight Line

**Have you observed dust particles in a sunbeam?** They seem to move in a completely jumbled fashion, darting about and suddenly changing direction. This motion, which seems to be random, is called Brownian motion, named after Robert Brown (1773–1858). However, it is not random. It is governed by the Laws of Motion, which were first written down by Isaac Newton after many years of observation and experimentation.

These laws form the basis of **mechanics**—the science of making things move. As we saw on page 5, every movement must have velocity and direction.

▲ *Brownian motion can be explained by Newton's Laws of Motion*

## 🔍 Newton's First Law of Motion

In simple language, this law says that an object will not change its state of motion on its own, unless some force acts upon it. An object has only two states of motion: at rest or moving in one direction. This is known as the Law of Inertia.

Imagine that you've gone to the edge of the solar system with your friends (no atmosphere, no gravity) to play cricket. Your friend bowls and you hit the ball hard. It will fly out of the solar system and to the end of the Universe. That's because the force of your hit gave it motion, and unless it crashes into something, there's no force to stop it. This won't happen on Earth because air **drag** will slow the ball down and gravity will pull it back to Earth.

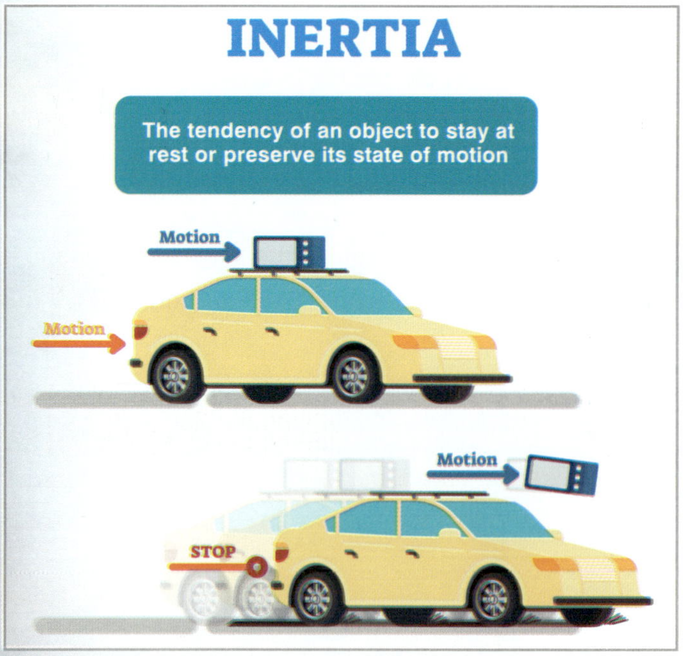

### INERTIA

The tendency of an object to stay at rest or preserve its state of motion

▲ *Things fall frontwards when you brake a moving car because of inertia*

## Newton's Second Law of Motion

This law says that the amount (magnitude) and direction of the net force ($F_{net}$) that acts on an object can be measured by:

1. the mass (m) of the object
2. the direction it moves in
3. the acceleration (a) it undergoes

Think of a football. When it's on the ground, it experiences several forces on it. When you kick it, your foot has to give it enough force to overcome gravity, normal force, friction force, and the drag due to air. The final acceleration of the ball is proportional to whatever is left of the force of your kick. Therefore,

$$F_{net} = ma$$

▶ *Understanding Newton's Second Law of Motion could help you win many football matches*

## Newton's Third Law of Motion

According to this law, for every force, there will be another force equal to it, which acts in the opposite direction. You have seen one such force—the normal force, which stops an object from crashing through the solid it is placed on. This force makes a ball bounce off the ground or the wall. When you drag something on the ground, the friction resists you. Another such force is **buoyancy**, which makes things float on liquids. When you dive into a pool, you can feel the water pushing you up. Yet another is drag, the friction caused by moving through a fluid.

◀ *When you hit a ball, you will experience recoil, the equal and opposite force to the ball hitting your bat*

# When Things Don't Move in a Straight Line

**Though we think of motion as something that goes in a straight line, there are other kinds too.** One of them is like the swaying of a clothesline, known as vibration. The movement of a swing is another kind of motion, called oscillation. The linear movement of an oscillating body is called **propagation**. When it moves forward while oscillating, we get a **wave**. The **rotation** of the Earth on its axis is circular motion; and the **revolution** of our planet around the Sun is combination of both linear and circular motions.

▲ *The pendulum of a grandfather clock oscillates, while the hands of the clock face rotate*

 ## Vibration

Vibration is the movement of an object around a mean position. When you pull the string of a violin and let it go, the string goes back to its resting state with some force. But its momentum is so much that the string goes right past the resting point to the other end, along the same distance as you pulled on the other side. As the string swings back, its momentum makes it go past the resting point again. This to-and-fro movement is called vibration. If there were no drag due to air, this would go on endlessly.

To vibrate, there has to be a motive force pulling the object away and a resisting force pulling it back to the original state. It is often the same force, which changes direction once the vibrating entity has reached one end. In a metal string, it is the **strain** (the extent to which the atoms can be pulled apart).

◀ *The energy of a vibrating string is transmitted to us as sound waves*

 ## Oscillation

When something moves and comes back to its place again and again, physicists say that it undergoes periodic motion. An object that vibrates with a defined time period is said to oscillate. That's how a playground swing works. At the subatomic level, everything oscillates—atoms, nuclei, electrons, quarks, and photons. The energy to oscillate comes from their electromagnetic field. Frequency is the measure of the number of oscillations a particle does in one second. It is measured in Hertz (Hz). Every particle has its own natural frequency of oscillation, which depends on the amount of energy it possesses.

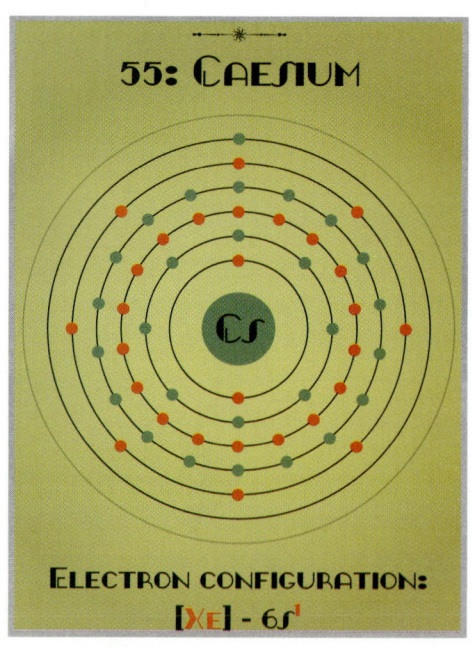

▲ *The oscillation of a Caesium-133 atom is used to define a 'second', the unit of measuring time*

# Wave Motion

A wave propagates when oscillating objects also move linearly. Waves are longitudinal, when the direction of propagation and oscillation are the same. Our ears catch longitudinal waves in the air as sound. In a transverse wave, the particles oscillate perpendicular to the direction of propagation. Light and radio waves travel this way.

▶ Types of waves

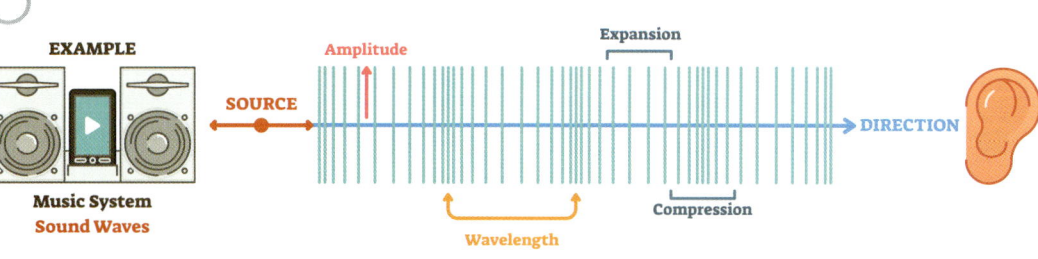

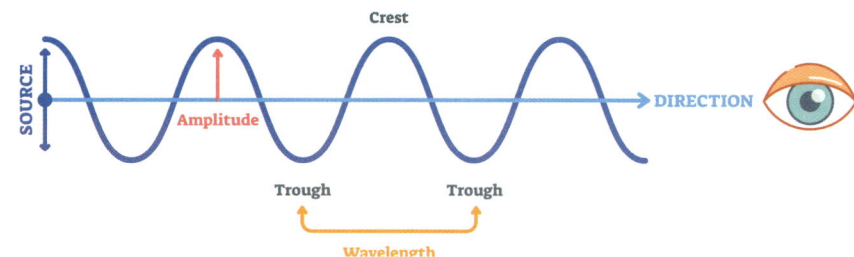

# Circular Motion

Circular motion is how a wheel or a disc moves. To calculate how fast a rotating or revolving object is moving, you must measure the angle it moves, not the distance. This measure is called **angular velocity** and it is measured in degrees per second. As the Earth rotates, all places on the same longitude have the same angular velocity. Nevertheless, they all have different linear velocities. If you stand at the Equator, you have 24 hours to cover 40,075 km, the circumference of the Earth. At the North or South Pole though, you don't have to move at all!

▼ *The angular velocity of a point on the edge of a wheel is the same as its centre. However, its linear velocity is much faster, as it has to travel the full circumference*

# In Real Life

All the members in a rock band use the power of oscillation to make music. The guitarists depend on the strain of their strings, the drummers on that of the membrane, and the singers, their own vocal chords!

▲ *Music depends on making a harmonious mix of the natural frequencies of all oscillating things*

# How the Planets Move

**Why do the planets all seem to go around the Sun in neat paths?** Nothing holds them in place after all, no rails or cables. They are actually held together by gravity and move according to special laws. Many of these laws were discovered by Johannes Kepler (1571–1630) after several years of observation of the night sky. Kepler's Laws are based on the **heliocentric theory**—the idea that the Earth goes around the Sun, and not, as it seems every day, that the Sun goes around the Earth.

## Kepler's First Law

**The orbit of every planet is elliptical with the Sun at one of its foci.**

Think of an ellipse as a stretched circle, so it would have two centres (called foci). Planets go around the Sun in a slightly elliptical orbit, not a round one. How much the orbit is off from being a full circle is called its orbital eccentricity (symbol e). For example, our Earth has an eccentricity of 0.017, while the dwarf planet Pluto, the most elliptical, has an eccentricity of 0.248 (it would be zero for a fully circular orbit). Because of this elliptical orbit, the Earth comes closest to the Sun on January 3 (called Perihelion) and moves the fastest, and goes farthest from the Sun on July 4 (called Aphelion) and moves the slowest. Planets (and moons) have elliptical orbits because they pull each other as well as the Sun. Planets change their eccentricity as they come closer or go farther from each other.

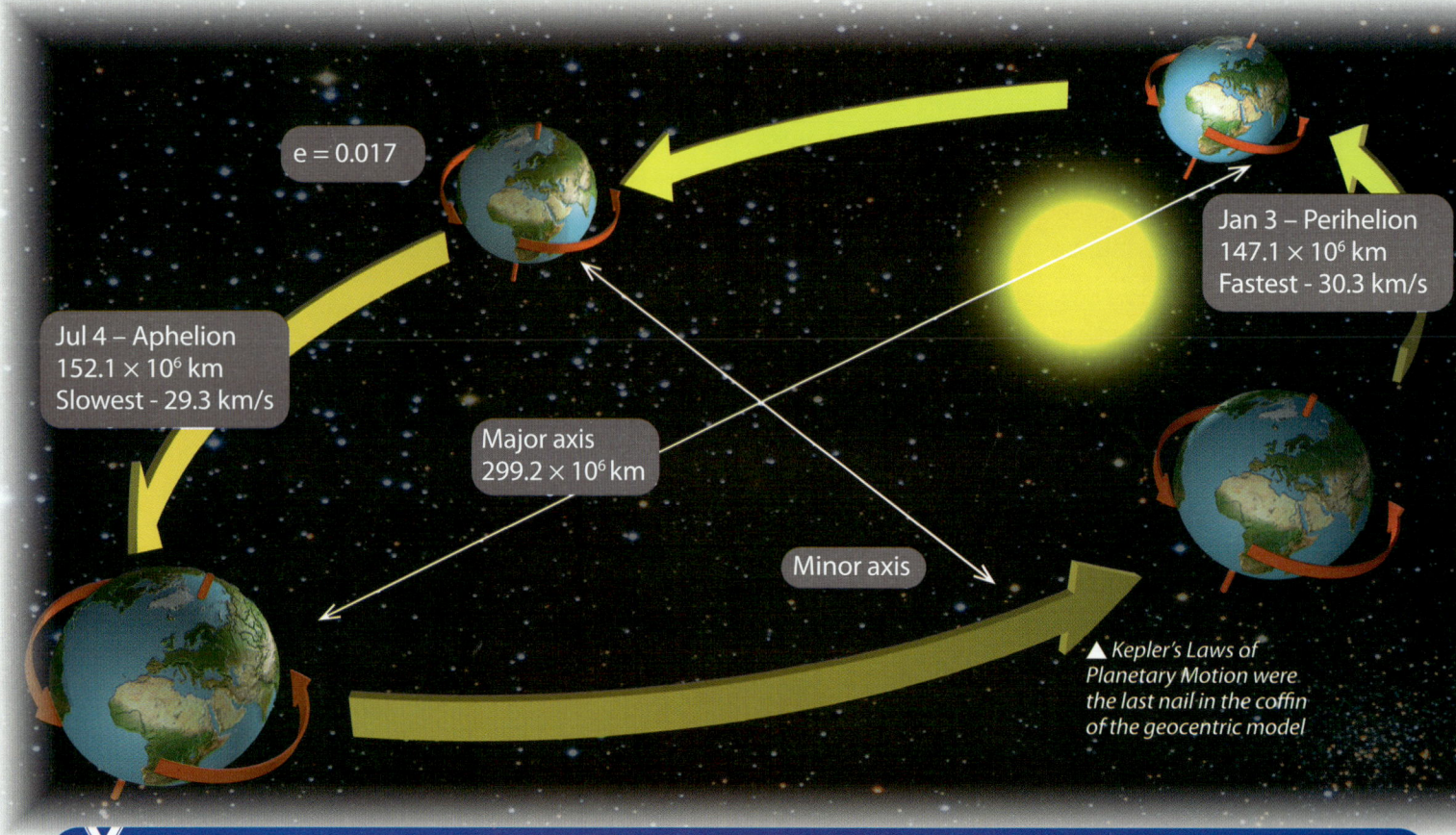

▲ Kepler's Laws of Planetary Motion were the last nail in the coffin of the geocentric model

## Incredible Individuals

For most of history, people thought that the Earth was flat and that it was the stars and other planets that went around it (**geocentric theory**). In Europe, the astronomers Nicolaus Copernicus (in 1543) and Galileo Galilei (in 1615) published their observations that suggested it was the Earth that went around the Sun instead, but they got in trouble with the Catholic Church for doing so. Only when Johannes Kepler provided a convincing mathematical explanation in 1609, did heliocentrism slowly get accepted.

▲ Galileo Galilei   ▲ Nicolaus Copernicus

▶ If you find a planet orbiting a distant star, you can find out its orbital period. Then, using Kepler's and Newton's Laws, you can find out its mass and orbit

## Kepler's Second Law

**A planet travels faster when near the Sun, and slower when farther.**

This is because gravity accelerates the planet as it comes closer to the Sun. The Earth takes 365 days to complete a trip around the Sun, so it clearly travels some distance each day. As it comes closer to the Sun, it covers a longer distance along its orbit, and as it goes farther away, it travels for a smaller distance.

## Kepler's Third Law

**The square of a planet's orbital period is proportional to the cube of half its major axis.**

A planet's **orbital period** is the time it takes to go around the Sun. The major axis is the longest line from the ends of the ellipse that runs through both foci. Astronomers use this law to calculate how long a planet will take to go around the Sun, if they know the major axis of its orbit. They then use this to know when the distance between our planet and another will be the smallest, which is useful for launching spacecrafts in order to minimize the distance to be traveled.

### Isn't It Amazing!

After Uranus was discovered in 1781, astronomical calculations of its orbit did not match observations, suggesting that another planet was interfering. In 1846, the French astronomer Urbain Jean Joseph Le Verrier (1811–77) calculated where this new planet could be. No French observatory agreed to look for it, so he wrote to Johann Gottfried Galle (1812–1910) at the Berlin observatory in Germany. His letter reached Galle on 23 September, 1846, and Galle found Neptune that very night!

▶ Neptune was discovered at a location just 1° off from where Verrier had said it would be

# Why Things Fall Down

When learning about gravity, you may come across a story that says that Isaac Newton discovered gravity when he was sitting under a tree and an apple fell on him. But the story of Newton's discovery is more complex than that. Let's talk about this discovery and how it changed the world.

> 💡 **Isn't It Amazing!**
>
> Did you know that the apple tree that inspired Newton still stands? It grows in Woolsthorpe Manor in Lincolnshire, England, which was Newton's childhood home, and is now over 350 years old.

## 🔍 Newton's Law of Universal Gravitation

Although we know that the Earth attracts all things to itself, Newton suggested that the reverse was also true: all things attract the Earth to themselves too. He figured out that the force of the attraction (symbol $F_g$) was proportional to the mass of the two bodies attracting each other (symbols $m_1$ and $m_2$), and inversely proportional to the square of the distance between them (r). Another factor is the gravitational constant (G), whose value is $6.673 \times 10^{-11}$ N m2/kg2.

$$F_g = \frac{Gm_1m_2}{r^2}$$

So, you could say that not only does an apple fall towards the Earth, but the Earth moves towards the apple too. But since the mass of the apple (a few grams) is nothing compared to the Earth's mass ($5.97 \times 10^{24}$ kg), and the distance between the Earth and the apple is only a tiny fraction as compared to the Earth's radius ($6.37 \times 10^6$ m or 6370 km), the force of attraction ($F_g$) between the apple and the Earth depends only on the Earth. Therefore, when you do the math, $F_g$ = 9.8 Newtons.

$$F_g = \frac{6.673 \times 10^{-11} \times 5.97 \times 10^{24}}{(6.37 \times 10^6)^2} = 9.8 \text{ N}$$

Now, from Newton's Laws of Motion, we know that F = mass (m) times acceleration (a). But since the mass is negligible, the acceleration due to gravity (g) is effectively a constant everywhere on Earth, that is, 9.8 m/s².

## 🔍 General Relativity

Over time, Newton's law has failed to explain many aspects of gravity. Albert Einstein proposed a radical new solution: space-time. Space-time is the fabric of the Universe, made of the three dimensions of space and one of time. Everything in space is embedded in space-time but huge objects such as planets and stars can bend it around them. To imagine how this happens, get your friends to stretch a cloth flat. Place a football on it. Doesn't it bend the sheet around itself?

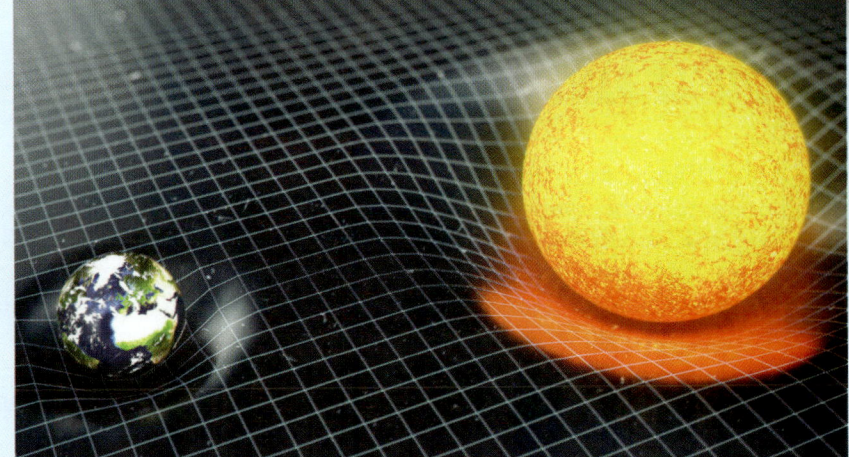

▲ The bending of space-time causes smaller objects to be drawn to the larger ones

SCIENCE | FORCE & MOVEMENT

▼ Gravity holds the solar system together

## 🔍 Gravitational Waves

Einstein's theory of space-time acting as a fabric means that it will have ripples going through it when something big happens (such as two stars crashing). These "ripples" are called **gravitational waves** and have the same speed as light. Unlike electromagnetic waves though, they are not known to be made of any particle till now.

▶ Gravitational waves were found by a special detector called LIGO in 2016—a hundred years after Einstein predicted them

## ⭐ Incredible Individuals

The Binomial theorem, laws of motion, force and mass, acceleration, inertia, universal gravitation, differential calculus, momentum, weight, vector addition, projectile motion, centripetal acceleration, circular motion, satellite motion, tidal forces, the precession of the equinoxes, and optics—one scientist discovered them all. His name is Isaac Newton, the Father of the Scientific Revolution.

▶ Newton humbly said of his discoveries, "If I have seen further, it is by standing on the shoulders of giants."

# Forces of Resistance

**When you pull a heavy box across the floor, why does it seem so hard to pull?** This is because of friction, which is a perpendicular force resisting your forward motion. Much of friction is caused by forces of **adhesion** between the atoms and molecules of the two solids in contact. As you saw on page 9, these are ionic attraction and van der Waals forces.

In reality, friction between two things should be small because their surfaces are not entirely smooth, even if they appear so. That's because they have microscopic hills and valleys called asperities. But when an object has been resting, the force of gravity (mg) works with the adhesive forces to pull it down and crush the asperities. In turn, this increases the surface of contact and the adhesion becomes stronger. That's why it's harder to make an object move than to keep it moving.

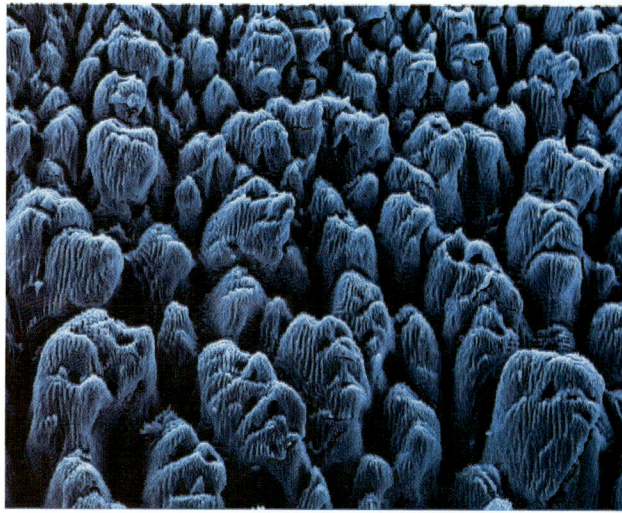

▲ *The surface of silicon, seen under an electron microscope. What looks smooth and shiny to the naked eye is in fact a microscopically rough surface*

## Friction

As friction depends on adhesive forces, it depends on the materials in contact. Physicists use a measure called the coefficient of friction (symbol $\mu$) to measure how two solids will interact. It is the ratio of the force required to pull (F), to the weight of the material (called load, L). Therefore, $\mu = F/L$. If the ratio is 1, it means as much force is needed to pull the load as its weight.

However, there are two coefficients of friction—one for calculating how much effort is needed to make a standing thing move (**coefficient of static friction**, symbol $\mu_s$) and one for keeping a moving thing moving (**coefficient of kinetic friction**, symbol $\mu_k$). To make a car that weighs 1,000 Newtons move, you will need 840 Newtons of force, but only 720 Newtons once it is moving. That's because the $\mu_s$ for friction between rubber (your car's tire) and concrete (the road's surface) is 0.84, while the $\mu_k$ is only 0.72.

▶ *When skating on ice, the steel blades need just 3 Newtons of force to move 100 Newtons of weight ($\mu_k = 0.03$)*

### In Real Life

Why can lizards stick to walls, ceilings, and even glass windows without falling? That's because their feet have hundreds of tiny hair. This increases the total surface in contact and the total van der Waals forces, and therefore increases friction.

▶ *Gecko legs maximise friction to the extent that their legs "stick" to walls*

#  Drag

Drag is the resistance that a fluid offers to a solid object moving through it. You feel drag when walking into the wind or while swimming. It depends on the density and viscosity of the fluid; the speed at which the object is moving; the area that's exposed to the fluid; and the shape of the moving object.

▼ *A bullet train's "nose" is designed to minimise the drag it faces while moving at high speed. This is called streamlining*

#  Viscosity of Fluids

Fluids (gases and liquids) have fewer atoms or molecules and therefore less cohesion. Nevertheless, they have some friction within them, called viscosity. Viscosity depends on how close the atoms or molecules are to each other. A thin liquid (like water) has low viscosity, while a thick liquid (like oil) has high viscosity. Viscosity decides how fast a fluid will "flow". The viscosity of a liquid decreases if you heat it, since its atoms or molecules go further apart.

▲ *If you cool honey in the fridge, it will become a lot more viscous*

#  Lubrication

Lubrication is a way to reduce friction between two solids, by introducing a liquid between them. The lubricant must have high viscosity to ensure that the friction between it and the solid surfaces does not tear it apart; otherwise, the solids will come in contact. Lubricants must also resist changing viscosity too much when they get heated in the process.

▲ *Lubricant in a machine makes sure that its gear wheels don't jam each other through friction*

# Machines

**The word 'machine' makes you think of things with a number of gears and screws and complicated moving parts.** But that's not what a machine means to physicists. To them, a machine is any device that transfers work done at one end (called the input work, $W_{in}$) to another end (the output work, $W_{out}$). Thus, in a robotic arm that's making a car, there will be a large number of tiny machines that make the whole arm, each transferring work till the end.

In an ideal machine, all the work would be transferred without loss of energy, but in the real world, there's always friction (because of solid parts touching each other) and drag (because of air). Therefore, the usefulness of a machine is measured in terms of Efficiency (η), the fraction of the input that is delivered as final work.

$$\eta = \frac{W_{out}}{W_{in}} = \frac{Energy_{out}}{Energy_{in}} = \frac{F_{out} * s_{out}}{F_{in} * s_{in}}$$

You read that work is the product of the force (F) and the length moved by the mass (displacement, s). So, if the displacement of the input can be doubled, the force can be halved. The ratio of the output force to the input force is called a mechanical advantage (MA).

$$MA = \frac{F_{out}}{F_{in}}$$

## Inclined Plane

This is the simplest machine in which one end is higher than the other. It is used to raise a load (P) for a distance (s), by actually dragging it at an angle, rather than pulling or pushing it upwards directly. The work done is the work required to overcome the pull of gravity. The smaller the angle of the incline (its **gradient**), the smaller the force required to counter the pull of gravity and raise the load. This is why we feel less tired going up a gentle slope than a steep staircase.

## Lever

A lever is a machine made of three parts: a load arm, an effort arm, and a fulcrum. The length of the two arms makes the most difference, as does the location of the fulcrum, which divides levers into three classes.

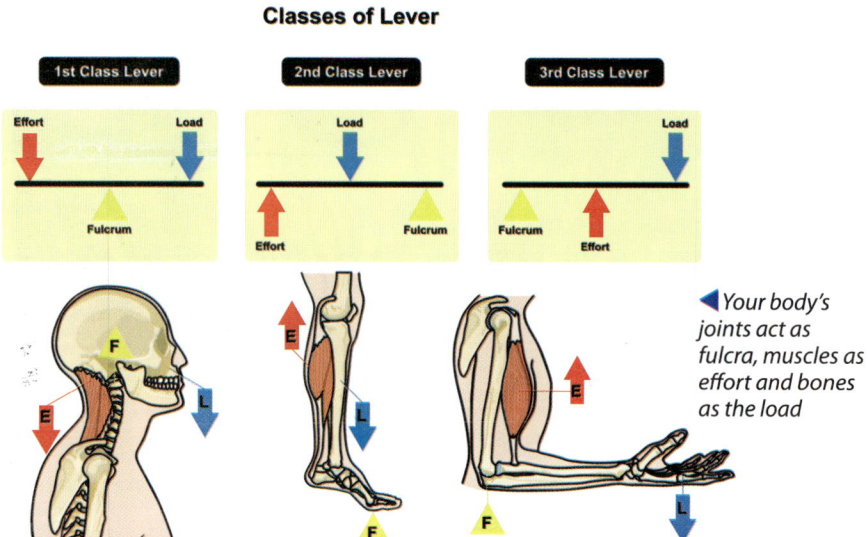

◄ Your body's joints act as fulcra, muscles as effort and bones as the load

### Isn't It Amazing!

Trains have difficulty going up mountains. As they have very little friction, they can slip on the tracks if the slope is too steep. They need to ascend as gradually as possible, so the track has to be laid so that it goes round and round the mountain, with many tunnels and bridges. This also reduces the force required to counteract gravity, making them go faster.

▲ The low gradient makes the train spend very little energy climbing

SCIENCE | FORCE & MOVEMENT

## Wheel and Axle

A wheel and axle convert linear motion into rotational motion, greatly minimising friction and increasing **efficiency**. The longer the radius of the wheel, the less effort you need to put in to move. You see this type of machine everywhere: in motor vehicles, in machines, in toys, and even the wheels of your suitcase!

▶ Cranes use a wheel and axle called a windlass to convert rotational motion into linear motion

## Pulley

A pulley is a wheel over which a cable runs carrying a load. The most common use of it is in an elevator, where a counterbalancing weight going down pulls the elevator car up.

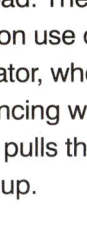

◀ By using a combination of pulleys, the length of the rope can be increased, so that the counterweight can be made lighter

## Wedge

A wedge turns the force applied in one direction by an angle. A knife is a good example of a wedge: by pressing your knife down on a carrot, you drive the two pieces away till they split. Humans have been making wedges since the Early Stone Age, in the form of stone axes and cutters.

▲ Pizza knives combine wedges and wheels

## Screw

A screw is an inclined plane (the ribs of the screw) arranged in a spiral around an axis, to convert rotational motion to linear motion. Screws are used in presses to crush things with little force.

▶ Screw-presses are used traditionally in Asia to press milk from coconuts

### ⊙ Incredible Individuals

James Starley (1830–1881) and his nephew John Starley (1854–1901) perfected the modern bicycle. Through a simple combination of pulleys, wheels, and levers, it efficiently converts your input (pedalling) into motion.

◀ All modern bicycles are based on Starleys' safety bicycle

# Density and Buoyancy

**Density (symbol d) is simply a measure of how much matter there is in a unit of space.** We use mass (m) as a measure of the amount of matter and volume (V) as the measure of space. Therefore, the formula for calculating density is simply:

$$d = \frac{m}{V}$$

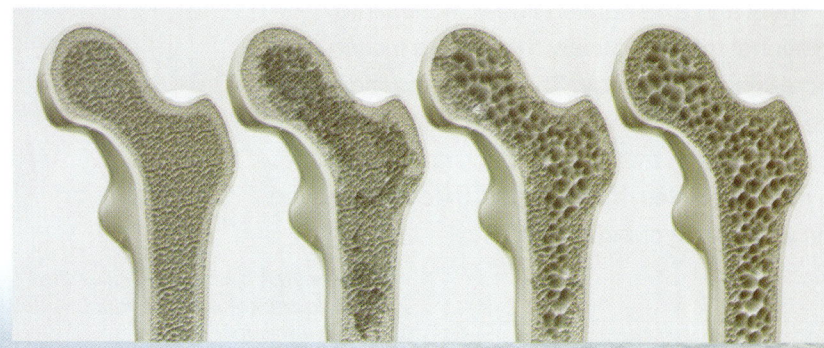

▲ As we age, our bone density reduces, making them prone to breaking

Density is expressed as kilogrammes per cubic metre ($kg/m^3$) or grams per cubic centimetre ($g/cm^3$). (These units are now the standard units throughout the world.) When the metric system was defined, the density of pure water at 4°C was fixed as 1 $g/cm^3$, and the densities of all other materials are compared to it **(relative density)**. Density is an important character of a substance and has a strong role in determining what that substance may be used for.

## 🔍 Floating and Sinking

Why do some things, such as iron nails, sink in water, while others, such as wooden nails, float? It is because of their density (d). Density increases the force on the object due to the Earth's gravity (g). The heavier mass will be pulled faster towards the Earth.

If you put an object in water, it will experience normal force that counteracts gravity, called buoyancy. Buoyancy is the resistance of the fluid to being displaced. The van der Waals forces between a liquid's atoms or molecules have to be broken by an object sinking through it (or in the case of a ship, moving horizontally). An object denser than water will have a force (m*g) strong enough to break through it, so it sinks. An object less dense (rarer) than water will not have enough force to break through, so it floats.

As gases have weaker van der Waals forces than liquid, they have lesser buoyancy and viscosity.

▶ Iron-bodied ships float because their hold is full of air (or crude oil), so that the total density is less than that of water

## Isn't It Amazing!

As air is heated, its molecules move away from each other, reducing its density. The buoyancy of the cooler air below will push it upwards. This is the principle used in flying hot air balloons. Helium and hydrogen are lighter than air, so balloons filled with them also float.

▶ Zeppelins are hydrogen balloons coupled with propellers. They were used for air transport in the early 20th century

## Specific Gravity and Purity

Relative density is the density of a substance expressed as a fraction of the density of a reference substance. When water is used, this is called **specific gravity**. This measure is used to determine whether an object is pure or contaminated, by the Archimedes Principle. If an object is put in water, it will displace water equal to its own volume. Two dense objects of the same weight will displace different volumes of water, which you can measure.

Gold is an expensive and very dense metal. It is often mixed with silver or copper for making jewellery and other things. If an object made of gold displaces more water (by volume) than a nugget of gold of the same weight, you know that it is impure.

▼ The purity of gold objects is measured in carats. 1 carat is equal to a gold content of 4.166% in the object

## Fresh Water and Seawater

Salt dissolved in water adds to its mass without changing its volume. That makes seawater, which is rich in salts, denser and therefore more buoyant than water in river deltas. Ships moving from freshwater ports to the open sea experience more buoyancy, while those moving in the reverse direction sink a bit.

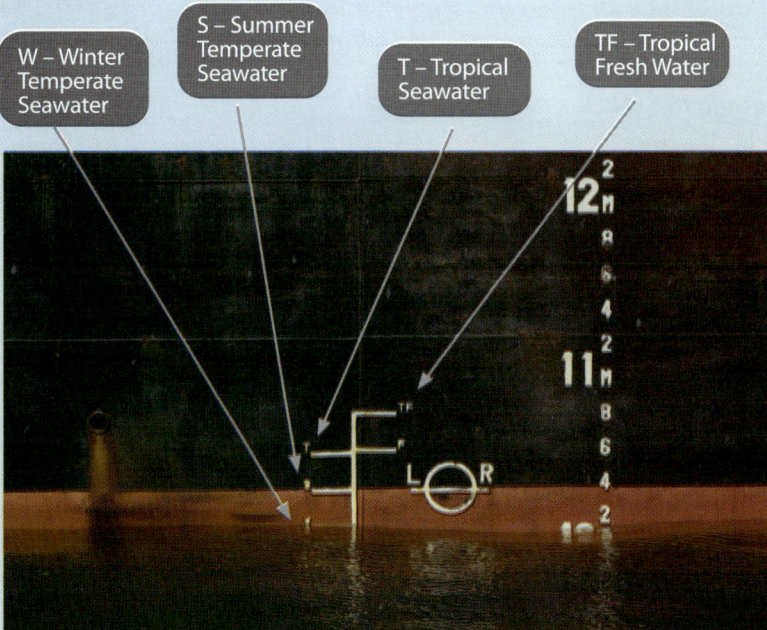

◀ Plimsoll Lines indicate how much a ship's hull may sink safely in fresh water and seawater in summer and winter. The numbers show the depth to which the ship's bottom (keel) has sunk below the surface

- W – Winter Temperate Seawater
- S – Summer Temperate Seawater
- T – Tropical Seawater
- TF – Tropical Fresh Water

# Engines

**Humans have always dreamed of mechanical motion.** One inventor attempted to use windmills as propellers to drive carts in 1714. Another one tried to run a car powered by wound-up clockwork in 1748. But neither were reliable.

During the Industrial Revolution, the science of converting heat energy into work (thermodynamics) was developed. Engineers wondered whether they could build practical engines that could actually do work, especially hauling loads of coal out of coal mines and carrying the loads into factories. Nicolas Cugnot built a steam-powered car in 1769 that could run for 20 minutes, but then had to rest for the next 20. Thomas Savery, Thomas Newcomen, James Watt, and Richard Trevithick, each one improved on the other's design of the steam engine, making them much lighter and faster. Other inventors, such as Karl Benz and Gottfried Daimler, both from Germany, worked on internal combustion engines, which were much lighter than steam engines.

▲ This exhibit in the Metiers Art Museum, Paris, is the world's oldest surviving motor vehicle, though some parts of it are new

## 🔍 Steam Power

Steam is full of energy, and if confined in a chamber, will try to push its way out. A piston is a lid, like a disc of metal, which can be used to make the chamber bigger or smaller. If the piston is attached to a rod, the force of the steam pushing against it can be converted into work. This is the idea behind a steam engine.

In the picture on the right, you see four stages of the engine at work. First, the steam is boiled and enters the piston chamber. As it enters, it pushes against the piston. As the energy is converted to mechanical energy that moves the wheel, the steam cools and is drained off. A second rod attached to the wheel controls a moving sluice. Once the piston is pushed to the end, the wheel has rotated half a circle. The rod now closes one inlet of steam and opens the inlet on the other end. Steam rushes into that side and pushes the piston back, completing one turn of the wheel. This is called a double-acting engine.

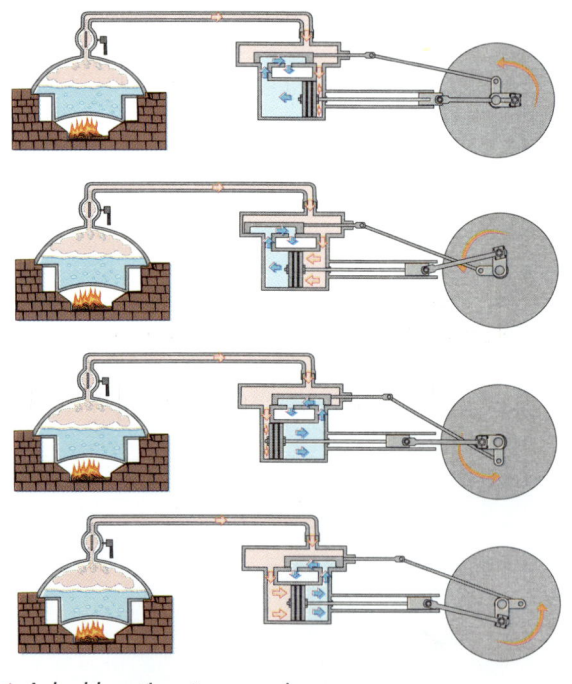

▲ A double acting steam engine conserves power and does nearly double the work

### 👁 In Real Life

As steam-powered engines were heavy, they were run on railroads, so that the iron wheels running on iron tracks would have minimum friction.

◀ Steel wheels on steel tracks allow really high speeds as rolling friction is near zero

SCIENCE | FORCE & MOVEMENT

## 🔍 Internal Combustion Engine

The weight of the water and the coal used to power the steam engine made it very heavy. What if the gas released as the fuel burns could be used to push the piston, instead of using steam? This is the idea behind the internal combustion engine.

Modern internal combustion engines have a piston chamber (cylinder) like steam engines. On the intake stroke (see 1 in the picture), the engine takes in air from the atmosphere and a small amount of fuel from the fuel tank. It compresses it in the compression stroke (2). In the power (or combustion) stroke (3), an electric spark ignites the fuel. The heat of the combustion causes the air to expand rapidly, pushing the piston forcefully. In the final exhaust stroke (4), the burnt fuel and air are removed from the cylinder.

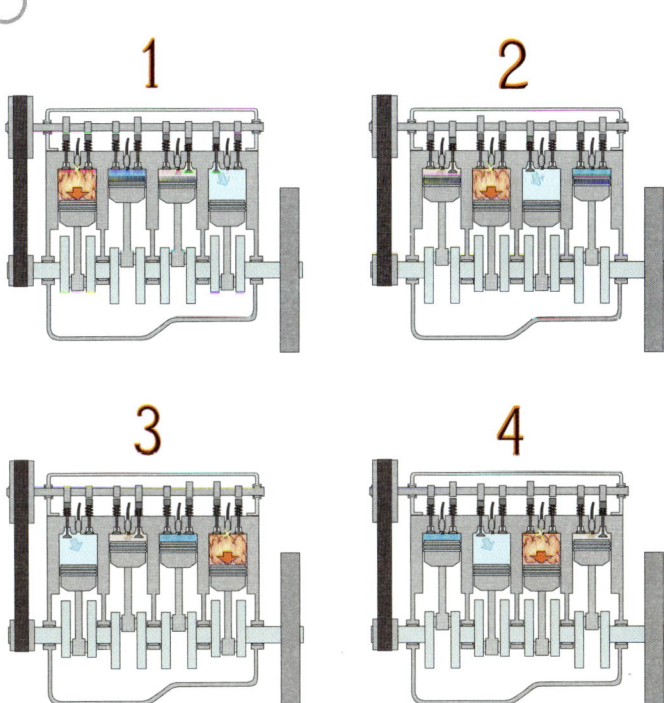

▲ Linking four cylinders in different stages produces a more efficient conversion of heat to work

◀ Belts connect the engine's crankshaft to the axles, so that the energy from the engine can be transmitted to the wheels as mechanical force

▼ The black cylinder is the steam boiler, while the black box below it, in front of the wheels, is the piston box

### ⭐ Incredible Individuals

Bertha Benz made the first long distance car journey with her sons Eugene and Richard in 1888 from Mannheim to Pforzheim in Germany. Her trip attracted crowds and people began to see the advantages of a lightweight self-powered carriage.

▲ Bertha Benz (left) and the BenzPatent Motorwagen (right). She was the main investor in her husband Karl Benz's factory, and also invented brake pads

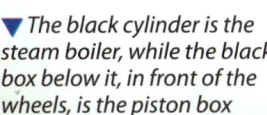

# Flight

**Humans have always wanted to fly.** Greek mythology tells the story of Daedalus, a talented artisan who, along with his son Icarus, was imprisoned by Minos, the king of the island of Crete. Daedalus made wings out of feathers and wax for himself and Icarus. As they flew out of prison, Icarus flew too close to the Sun, whose heat melted the wax. Icarus fell into the sea and drowned.

The only problem with this invention is that humans don't have the bones or the muscles needed to fly, even if we make better wings. But we can use the power of physics to make flying devices, and we'll learn about them here.

◀ *The Fall of Icarus, painted by Jacob Peter Gowy, in the Museo del Prado, Madrid, Spain*

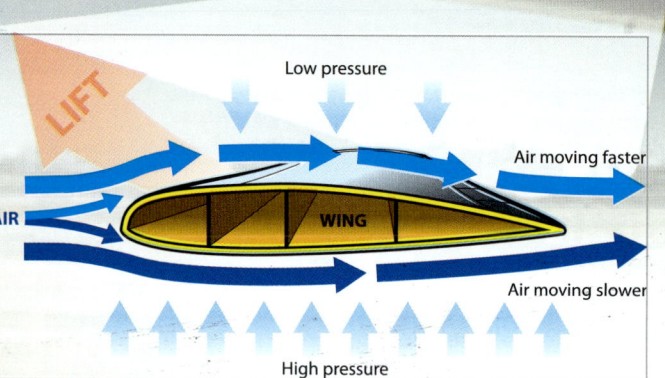

◀ An aerofoil is a special design that makes planes fly if they move very fast

## Lift

You've read how balloons fly using buoyancy. But there's another way, which scientists have known for centuries, called the **lift**. An object experiences drag caused by viscosity when moving through a fluid. As the object moves forward, it displaces the fluid, causing it to turn. This turn causes lift, a force that acts perpendicular to drag.

A special design of plane wings, called an aerofoil, ensures that lift acts upwards while the plane is moving forward. It makes use of the tiny differences in air pressure created by the aerofoil design, so that air is of lower pressure and higher speed above, and higher pressure and lower speed below. The difference in pressures pushes the wings upward. The faster the plane, the higher the lift. Planes at take-off need to have high velocity, so they have to speed up on a runway.

### Incredible Individuals

The first woman to get a pilot's license and fly on her own was Raymonde de la Roche of France. She got her license on 8 March, 1910; just six years after the Wright brothers made the first aeroplane flight on 17 December, 1903.

▲ *In 1919, Raymonde de la Roche flew a plane 16,000 feet above sea level, setting a world record*

SCIENCE | FORCE & MOVEMENT

## 💡 Isn't It Amazing!

If a propeller can fan air downwards, the thrust becomes the same as lift, so the plane rises. This is the basis of a helicopter.

▲ *The horizontal propeller provides lift, while the vertical propeller in the tail prevents the helicopter from spinning*

## 🔍 Propellers

If you jump off a cliff using a glider, the buoyancy of the air will keep you up while the lift is being generated. But for airplanes, a more reliable way is required. After many attempts by many people, the Wright brothers got it right. They perfected a screw propeller, which has twisted aerofoil blades. When it rotates, it fans air behind it, so the pressure in front reduces and that behind increases. This pressure difference pushes the plane forward very fast (thrust).

▶ *Propellers can be used to create thrust (forward) or lift (upward)*

## 🔍 Jet Propulsion

If you force water out of a garden hose at top pressure, you can feel the pushback (Newton's Third Law of Motion). This is the principle of the **jet**. A jet engine is an internal combustion engine paired with an air compressor. Compressed air meets the burning fuel and is pushed out through a turbine. As it rapidly expands in the atmosphere, it generates a huge amount of thrust.

▶ *Jet engines team up with aerofoils to create thrust and lift that power modern long-distance flight*

# To Space

**Getting to space has been a human dream for millennia.** It finally came true between 9:07 am and 10:55 am (Moscow time) on 12 April 1961, when Yuri Gagarin orbited the Earth. But how did he get there? What was the science that made it possible?

Getting to space involves a lot of really simple physics. You have to achieve escape velocity ($v_e$) to beat the Earth's gravity to get out there. You have to learn to build spacecrafts that are powerful enough to go a long, long way. You have to understand how to use gravity to give the spacecraft a boost.

## Thrust

You saw how planes rise by generating lift on pages 26–27. However, the lift is not enough to get a rocket to achieve escape velocity. So, it uses another principle called **thrust**. Thrust is the force with which the rocket pushes against the Earth first, and as it lifts off, against the air. A rocket must have enough thrust to beat drag, weight, and the potential energy it will keep gaining as it rises. Most rockets generate thrust by jet propulsion.

## Escape Velocity

Newton's Laws of Motion tell you that things accelerate as they fall to the Earth because of the Earth's gravitational pull (symbol g). As you go higher into the atmosphere (h), your potential energy rises too. For a rocket to beat this, it must have kinetic energy ($\frac{1}{2}mv^2$) equal to or more than the potential energy due to gravity (mgh) that it will acquire as it rises. It must therefore go fast enough to overcome this pull. To escape from Earth, you need to shoot out at 11 kilometres per second. And that's before taking into account the friction of the atmosphere.

$$\text{If } \tfrac{1}{2}mv^2 \geq mgh \text{ then } v_e = \sqrt{2gh}$$

### ⭐ Incredible Individuals

French satirical writer Savinien Cyrano de Bergerac (1619–1655) imagined curious ways of flying to the moon in his novel *Comical History of the States and Empires of the Moon*. He imagined an engine consisting of concave mirrors, which focus sunlight onto the air in it, making it rush out of the engine like a jet.

▶ *Savinien Cyrano de Bergerac also suggested that one could travel towards the Moon by tying bottles of dew to oneself*

## In Real Life

At orbital velocity, you can neither escape a planet (or a star) nor crash into it. Therefore, you end up going in circles, like the Moon goes around the Earth, or the Earth goes around the Sun.

▲ The moon's orbital velocity is 1.022 km/s

## Gravity Assist

As a spacecraft approaches a planet, it will accelerate due to that planet's gravity. If it is moving fast enough already, it can reach the escape velocity of that planet, with which it can shoot out further into space. Most crafts going to outer space use the Moon to do this.

▲ The Moon has no atmosphere because its escape velocity is less than that of gas molecules heated by sunlight

## Materials Science

The lighter the weight of the rocket and more powerful the fuel, the faster the thrust can take the rocket up. Therefore, most of 'rocket science' is really about fuel efficiency and learning how to build lighter rockets. Rockets are often made of high strength, low weight alloys. They are coated with ceramics so that the drag due to the atmosphere does not burn them up (this is especially important for returning spacecrafts).

Fuels (called propellants) are usually solids stored at very cold temperatures, so they take up less space and more can be filled in.

# The Metric System

**All the measurements you have seen in this book are expressed in units of the metric system.** But did you know that there are many other systems in the world for measuring length, area, mass, volume, force, etc.? Though almost all countries use the metric system now, the USA still largely uses the Imperial System.

The metric system originated in France after the 1789 French Revolution. The new Republican government was concerned that the hundreds of systems of weights and measures used in different parts of France would cause a lot of confusion. To address this, the government created a new system whose units of length, volume, mass, and time would be based on properties of nature itself. Everything would be based on the metre, which is how the system got its name.

The metre was to be one-ten-millionth (1/10,000,000) of the longitudinal distance from the North Pole to the South Pole. The gram would be the mass of one cubic centimetre of water at its maximum density, and the litre would be one-thousandth of a cubic metre. In 1799, a platinum block measured to be one kilogram and a platinum-iridium rod measured to be 1 metre became the standards by which all measuring and weighing devices were to be calibrated.

◀ This block of platinum was the international prototype of the kilogram till 20 May 2019, after which the weight was defined by the Planck's constant

## Metric Scale

The great advantage of the metric system is that it follows the decimal system, so that the calculation of units becomes easy. Greek prefixes are used for multiples of the metre, gram and litre, and Latin ones for fractions. This way, 100 metres is a hectometre, a million litres is a megalitre and one-tenth of a gram is a decigram.

| Prefix | Size in meters | Examples |
|---|---|---|
| Exa (E) | 1 quadrillion | 105 light years |
| Peta (P) | 1 quadrillion | ten light years |
| Tera (T) | 1 trillion | one light-hour |
| Giga (G) | 1 billion | the Sun |
| Mega (M) | 1 million | dwarf planet Ceres |
| kilo (k) | 1000 | Sydney Harbour bridge (length) |
| hecto (h) | 100 | football field |
| deca (da) | 10 | school bus |
|  | 1 | walking stick |

| Prefix | Size in meters | Examples |
|---|---|---|
| deci (d) | 1/10th | compact disk |
| centi (c) | 1/100th | children's fingers (width) |
| milli (m) | 1/1000th | flea |
| micro (µ) | 1-millionth | red blood cell |
| nano (n) | 1-billionth | DNA (width) |
| pico (p) | 1-trillionth | X-ray wavelength |
| femto (f) | 1-quadrillionth | atomic nucleus |
| atto (a) | 1-quadrillionth | quarks |

# SI Units

In 1875, the International Bureau of Weights and Measures was established in Sèvres near Paris, and other countries began to adopt the metric system. In 1960, a few changes were made to clear the confusion amongst scientists, and the new system was named the *Système Internationale* (French for 'International System'). It replaced the old definitions with those based on absolute, unchanging properties of nature, because many of the original standards changed over time.

The metre is now defined as the distance light travels in a vacuum in 1/299,792,458th of a second, since the speed of light in vacuum (symbol c) is exactly 299,792,458 m/s.

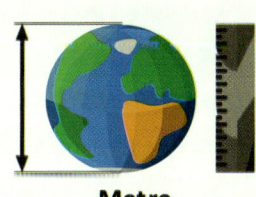
Metre

The kilogram is defined using the values of metre and second, and the Planck's constant (symbol h), whose value has been determined to be precisely $6.626,070,15 \times 10^{-34}$ kgm²/s. Therefore,

$$1 \text{ kg} = \frac{(299,792,458)2}{6.626,070,15 \times 10^{-34} \times 9,192,631,770} \text{ hs/m}^2$$

Kilogram

The second is equal to the duration of 9,192,631,770 periods of the radiation corresponding to the transition between the two hyperfine levels of the unperturbed ground state of one atom of Caesium-133 undisturbed by any other radiation.

Second

The Kelvin, the SI unit of temperature, is defined using the other three (metre, kilogram, and second), and the Boltzmann constant (symbol k), whose value has been determined to be $1.380,649 \times 10^{-23}$ kgm²/s²K. Therefore,

$$1 \text{ K} = \frac{1.380,649 \times 10^{-23}}{6.626,070,15 \times 10^{-34} \times 9,192,631,770} \text{ kgm}^2/\text{s}^2$$

Kelvin

▲ The Système Internationale defines seven basic units, from which all others are derived

The ampere is the unit of electric current, and is expressed as the amount of electrical charge (written in Coulombs) that passes through a conductor in 1 second. Its definition is based on the charge of the electron, which has been fixed as $-1.602\,176\,634 \times 10^{-19}$ Coulombs. 1 Ampere is 1 Coulomb per second.

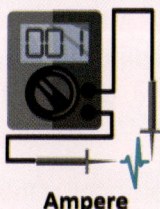
Ampere

The mole is the unit for the amount of a substance (n), which is a measure of the number of elementary entities such as atoms, molecules, ions, electrons, or subatomic particles. One mole is defined as exactly $6.02214076 \times 10^{23}$ elementary entities. This number is called the Avogadro number.

Mole

The candela is the SI unit for luminous efficacy (the scientific way to refer to 'brightness') of light sources in a given direction, such as an electric bulb or the Sun. One candela is defined as 1/683rd of the luminous efficacy of electromagnetic radiation of frequency $540 \times 10^{12}$ Hz in one direction.

Candela

### Isn't It Amazing!

The French also divided the circle into 400 degrees, instead of 360 degrees. Though it made calculations easier, people never adopted this system.

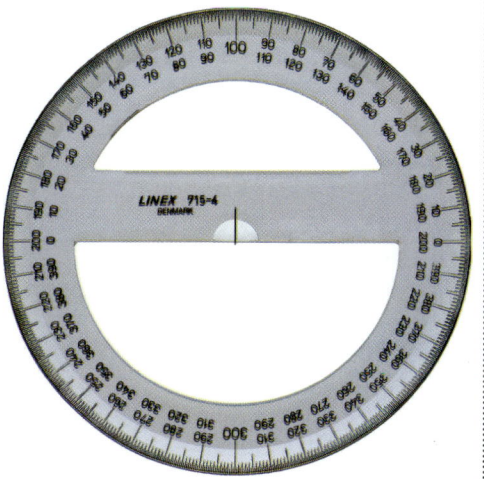

▲ A protractor showing metric and common degrees. (Licensed from Wikinger under the Creative Commons Attribution-Share Alike 3.0 Unported license.)

# Word Check

**Adhesion:** The forces that pull atoms or molecules of two substances together

**Angular Velocity:** The velocity with which an object traverses an arc of a circle

**Buoyancy:** The force exerted by a fluid resisting the force of gravity

**Coefficient of Kinetic Friction:** A measure of how much force will be needed to overcome friction between two substances moving in opposite directions

**Coefficient of Static Friction:** A measure of how much force will be needed to overcome friction between two substances resting on each other

**Dark Matter:** Matter whose particles are not organised into atoms, so they cannot interact with photons

**Density:** The mass of an object in a unit volume

**Displacement:** The difference between the initial and final locations of an object

**Drag:** Friction caused by an object moving through a fluid

**Efficiency:** The fraction of the input energy that a system delivers as work

**Energy:** The ability of a system to do work

**Experiences:** The effect of an external force upon an object

**External Work:** The work done by a system on the environment

**Friction:** The resistance offered to motion by electromagnetic attraction between objects

**Friction Force:** The force needed to overcome friction

**Geocentric Theory:** The theory that the Earth is at the centre of the Solar System

**Gradient:** The ratio of the rise of a plane and its horizontal length

**Gravitational Waves:** Disturbances in space-time caused by the movement of astronomical bodies

**Heliocentric Theory:** The theory that the Sun is at the centre of the Solar System

**Inertia:** An object's innate resistance to a force acting on it

**Internal Work:** The work done within a system

**Jet:** A fast-moving fluid which generates thrust because of its velocity

**Kinetic Energy:** The energy a system possesses because of its motion

**Lattice:** The pattern of arrangements of atoms, ions or molecules in a crystalline solid

**Lift:** A force exerted by a fluid at right angles to an object moving through it

**Light Matter:** Matter whose particles are organised into nuclei, electrons, and atoms, which can interact with photons

**Mass:** The amount of inertia in a system at rest, proportional to the number of particles in it

**Mechanics:** The science of motion and forces

**Momentum:** The amount of inertia in a body due to its mass and velocity

**Normal Force:** The force exerted by a solid resisting a substance pushing against it

**Orbital Period:** The time taken by an object to go around another object (for instance, a planet around the Sun or a satellite around a planet)

**Order of Magnitude:** The approximation of a measure in units of ten: tens, hundreds, thousands, etc.

**Potential Energy:** The energy available in a system for conversion to work

**Possession:** The physical attributes innate to an object

**Propagation:** The forward movement of an oscillating particle

**Relative Density:** The ratio of the density of a substance to the density of a reference substance

**Revolution:** Circular motion of an object about another object

**Rotation:** Circular motion of an object around its own axis

**Scalar:** A physical measure with magnitude but no direction

**Specific Gravity:** The ratio of the density of a substance to the density of water

**Strain:** The resistance a solid offers when pulled

**Thrust:** The reaction force offered by the ground when something pushes against it

**Van der Waals Force:** The attraction between atoms and molecules of a substance due to minor electric charges on them (electric dipole)

**Vector:** A physical measure with magnitude and direction

**Velocity:** The rate at which a body moves in one direction

**Wave:** The path of a moving, oscillating particle

**Weight:** The force on a body because of its mass and the Earth's gravitational pull